The Seeing Song of
Alan

2014

by
Alan Blair Ritter
12/3/2014

Acknowledgements:

I have a deep sense of gratitude to my parents and every one who let me be so naive about my self and the world for so long. It has been an interesting time. I would also like to thank directly the ladies that are supporting this reboot: Danuta Burnat and Christy Parry.

I would also like to acknowledge Jeff Starbuck aka Ram Das for his whispering of Rumi and Hafiz in my ear. That was really all that was necessary.

There have been so many teachers along the way in all the classrooms and fields, but I choose to let them know I love them without calling them out.

Finally, I would like to thank the kind reader for finding this document and thinking it might have something interesting to say. It does, but it may not say something you will like.

Table of Contents

The Foundation:

The Basic Human Condition

is

Bliss.

This is easily demonstrated.

Humans begin soul existence with a blank soul. Each and every step in experience adds to the record appearing on that soul. This record is a complete writing of everything going on in the Universe as well as all impressions and impacts of each instant. This record causes growth in the individual and guides the individual to look for other experiences once the experience genre being acted in pales and no longer provides as much expansion.

There are no events offered to humans that do not expand their soul. As such each and every experience is "building" a "more" experienced soul. You are broader or "more" experienced as a result of every single act you take part in. No exceptions.

There are no actions that are compressing. They are not offered. They serve no purpose. It is not possible to "erase the record." It is also not reasonable to want to erase the hard earned expansionary experience.

** Out beyond the notions of "good" (experience), and the notions of "bad" experience, there is a field. I will meet you there. -- Rumi **

This expansion is all that is going on every instant. It is all that can

5

go on.

It is bliss. It is constant. It does not change. It does not become something else.

It does not change and become "good" or "bad" according to some short lived society or philosophical rules that were made up yesterday.

Ever.

It is love. On all the time. Forever.

If my next action is bliss. What about the impact of my next action on someone else?

It can only be blissful for them. By definition.

By defintion, there is no karma. There is no loosing. There is only winning.

For everyone.

The need is to expand the palate beyond the moralistic "bad" and "good" to understand the nature of "I need to do that" regardless of what "that" is.

The Complexity of Consciousness

The soul is viewed as a record of what is.

This record is a record of all of the impressions, including every nuance of real and imagined action at every instance. An infant begins to build their "response to the world" or ego early on (depending on the development they came "in" with). This ego is a record of observations of events, impressions of how each "person" dealt with the events, and the preceived impact of the "person's" actions on their "status" with respect to those events, a "the Universe did this, the person did that, and the Universe handed them this reward as a result." So your friend Johnny screamed and cried when his parents drove past the Dairy Queen and in response they turned around and went back. Johnny got exactly what he wanted and his parents indulged themselves and you as well. This might be an interesting behavior for the future, but it might also play along the lines of whether you are interested in being like Johnny's family or not.

It does not matter that there are an infinite number of such events going on at any one time. The soul records them all. So the soul is literally the record of the mass action / behavior / psycho drama as it unfolds, from a being's perspective, instant after instant. It is interesting to realise that this soul is building (or building upon) a "reaction" center for personal goals or ego. So the original programming or person "type" that "you" are weighs the behavior inputs and incorporates what fits in. It is not a blank slate when it has been written on before (obviously).

This is a very complex record. A very complex process. And a very complex outcome.

Depending on the "length of the internal record" already in existence, it can be instructive to delve within for entertainment purposes. Not for "enlightenment" but merely for entertainment. It is just a record, complex, but just a record. It is how you use it to strive in the outside world that makes the difference.

The Status:

Endless Empire, Continuous Conquest and Feeding

It is endless, relentless, and everywhere.

The military business machine. The local actor (president), the local propaganda wing (media), the endless rain of useless work and food [make parts, make numbers, make already invented technologies, research solved problems, revolution (circles and circles and circles), build and demolish and build and demolish, etc.], carve up an illusory planet.

But it is not the daily activity that is the issue. It is realizing that it is endless and useless and self destructive, but not self destructive.

It instructs to realize when you have completed a task.

Because if you catch yourself doing a repetitive task you have never done before and you know it does not feel right to continue with the world as it is.

Behavior within the Conqueror Society

Each and every endeavor within the conqueror society is of the same type. The homogenization of the different, the coopting of what won't change, the annihilation of what won't be homogenized or coopted, and always and forever playing to the lowest common denominator.

Buy and throw away. All flavors and scents of the "real world" are duplicated and made kool aid like, then the real world equivalent is eaten and remembered deep in the past through the sickly sweet pseudo taste.

What was free for sweat and a little care, is now from 4,500 miles away from the Town Safe Factory. It wasn't safe to have it unregulated, we all feel much better that we never have to take responsibility for growing it anymore. You saw what happened last time "that guy" tried it? I am so safe with my plastic packets of flavors.

(How many layers of "real world" have we descended through? Lots?)

The tides of eating swirl on the planet. Forests are eaten. Oceans are eaten. The Earth itself is turned over and eaten. People are eaten. All the critters are eaten. But we "can't get me no satisfaction, no, no, no...no." The internal hunger never reasons to grow and only eat what is grown. Growing ourselves would show us the end of the trail, our own responsibility, our own hand. We must never lift a finger, "someone else" has to do all the work. Or we will take our ball and go home.

It has been long, long, and long living and knowing the role of Conqueror The-Rapist. For long, long, and long I have not learned anything new. Neither have my brothers and sisters. Is it time to leave?

Seeing the behavior, remember the things that are eaten? Are they gone? Never to be seen again? Lost?

They are not lost.

They are recorded in our souls. Every facet and detail. And all we need to do is focus and walk toward them. And they will be again.

We are that.

The verdant forests and grassy plains dotted with buffalo. We know what is necessary to get them back. Walk the path with heart. (Heart: move the h to the end is Earth.)

Or conversely, how many interations of lazing in conquest and constriction have we accomodated and still think it is acceptible. More, more, more!

Commercial Enterprise in the Company Town

Long ago it was writ that: "You are what you eat." So if I can market what you eat. etcetera.....

All forms of things to consume are too important to the illusionary space you are being frog marched into by the company town to be left to chance.

Music, News, Politics, Food, Water, Clothing, Sex, Religion, Yoga, Meditation, Exercise, Fast Food, etcetera....

Please (drool) with me (ahem) I mean have an exciting original (TM) life.

They will alter the price of their main hook items so that you can afford to be a client. Lower, lower, and lower. Eat, drink, and be merry.

Forget all your troubles. Watch the new happy happy comedy hour.

But it is the troubles and the itch that is humanity and the growth.

Dull that out with prescription meds and surgery.

Cut that painful !!!! right on out.

I don't want to feel pain anymore.

I don't want to feel at all.

Ever

Again.

And its all free, free, free!

What a bargain!

lol.

You can pay with your continuing custom.... .... and you do.

Are the walls closing in? No its getting better, more channels on the box, but less fish in the sea. Trees in the woods. Birds on the breeze. But better games in the box. Singers with the X-factor. !!! Uh-huh.

Packaged and known end of life makes me feel so secure and loved. How about you?

I went to the mortuary (grocer) and bought my meat and potatoes. I am planning ahead for exactly how I want to transition.

Who are we?: Clients of conquerors

I am a child of descendents of immigrants to the USA. As such I am a displaced "Euro" "Pean." You're a peon. Exactly. That.

But more exactly a soldier who is attracted by economic opportunity (as a bee to nectar). This is a marketed attraction unless you are completely aware (and most aren't). That marketed attraction is created by the conquerors. They are using the worker bees (beings in their marketed life style already) to move into a new geographic area and displace a native population. Who even knew they were there?

All we ever saw was the cute pictures of pilgrims eating Thanksgiving dinners with the "uncivilized" "half-naked" "alien-shaped" natives. They are not like us. Ignore them.

The thing is they are like us. How we used to be. Untold generations before. Many lifetimes ago for some. Before the empire rolled over our homeland using client slaves of their lifestyle. Just like us, now.

That is one reason why you are so insensitive to the latitudes taken by the conquestadors, the "white" fathers, the slaver owners, to the native population. Because it is too painful to look into your own heart. Cause it's you. But its a "you" that you are not dealing with.

The you that is too painful to deal with. How many times did you or your ancestors say: "I will kill myself rather than eat another shit meal provided by the Master"? How many times did the Master stick his penis in your ass? And it got to be so horrible that you forgot about it.

11

And the fact that you forgot about it so much that it still there and you don't feel it.

Taxes. Shit Food, Useless pointless work. To earn their paper. To buy more shit food and go to their schools. To walk endlessly into the facade of a silver screen they provide.

Pounding on the QWERTY keyboard. Or shoveling the mountain top until the Mother's creation is in the oven. Along with your self respect.

Is it an endless road? Or is taking it coupled with being the bully Master an endless relationship, never to be transcended?

See the "halves" (victim and assaultor) of the relationship and instantly see other possibilities to be explored.

Be not the victim or the assaultor. Or if you are in "customer service" then be what is required by the situation as it is required by each person you meet. If you are that conscious.

Are you that conscious?

How many generations ago was your native stock swept into being a client? How many empires have swept over your homeland denigrating what you thought was a native culture but turned it into an empire client of some sort?

And in this endless conquest, how many times have you been the conqueror? Holder of the sword for the Master? Or even having a go at being the Master? Being the planner of strategies of subjugation.

Not just a few times. A lot of times.

To get to a point where you look away and don't feel it. And eat animals, but feel love only for your pets. It is not love you feel for your pets. It is a pale imitaton. Because your love is not universal for everything. Your love is buried deep in your soul.

And its ok. It is a step on the path. It is necessary to build your armor so that you can be the angel of redemption. Or to be able to be in customer service as a conscious being.

Being non-feeling as the victim in an instant and the assaultor the next instant. The classic definition of a psychopath. Endlessly trapped as a victim and victimizer. Until your feelings come back.

And you transcend and become an angel in customer service.

There are not a few avenues to get your wings on. Lots of streets and alleys to explore. Lots of "pain" to "deal" and to "feel." Until you see it all as the same.

Customer Service

Diversity of Customer Service Offering

Customer Service is not swayed by good and bad, morality is meaningless.

Customer Service is a selection of services that can be offered in a given environment in such a way that all services are compatible in a side-by-side fashion, forming a society. Sometimes services are available side-by-side but some services are passcode protected (only "card" holders or "qualified" persons can access them). The former services are accessed by power or material wealth, etc. Merit or record services are only accessible due to inherent qualifications of the being under consideration.

In certain situations diversity dives toward a low number due to actions of higher level managers who are driving. Under these circumstances it is a circumstance of who is on hand and what they wish for as far as the outcome of events.

I know there are many higher functioning beings present here now in this space.

And I care about everyone.

But there is a driving passion that I have now.

Who and what am I?

My soul record is how long? How much is in there? Does everyone out "there" have this much in "here?"

Don't you wonder these things as well?

Isn't the most of your day inside rather than outside? Just naturally due to the weight of the soul and the little bit of an opening you have made to its record.

I see the customer service diversity dive just like you do. It bothers me too. But it was this dive that caused me to see inside in the first place, so I don't take it as a fault.

Do you mind terribly if I sit down and unpack?

All of it?

Don't you feel the same?

That it is time for a siesta from the laurel wreath gang (banksters) for the able?

From the cedar mushroom cultivators, who try so hard to get to God by dosing? Instead of hard work?

They are ok, too.

Script Connections:

Fuk-U-Shima:

Fuk

U

Shima

Shima means mother in Navajo. The rest can be read in "English" and is obvious.

The background for the issue is how long ago did the planning take place (was the script written) that would allow the name of a town in "Japanese" to read as the above epithet directed to the Earth in "English?"

Do you like living in a scripted world? Or do you like the script that is being written? Its a BBC teledrama.

Emmaus is a small town in Pennsylvania, United States of America. It is adjecent to Allentown, which is next to Bethlehem. Bethlehem has significance that is well known. But the humble EM MAUS may have more. Because an M Mouse is a lettered laboratory animal, a test subject. A little white mouse.

In modern culture you know three huge corporate M Mice. They are Mickey, Minnie, and Mighty.

Emmaus, Pennsylvania was incorporated in 1756. This is an idea of the scripting timelines. It is all written out a *long* *time* ago. The script might as well have been written at time *zero.* What events are not in the script? What events are in the script? Are your thoughts and impulses in the script? Who wrote the script?

Does not matter who wrote it. To know it exists is enough.

In the local region of Emmaus a family of folks has been living for many years. Their family name is Serfass. Their family name is Serf-Ass, Serf Ass. Emmaus is a Borough, a designation of a small town. A borough can also be pronounced Burrow or Burro. The former is an animal home dug into the ground and the later is an Ass, a beast of burden.

So there is a burrow of M Mouse in which Serf Ass(es) labor? No explanation is needed. Is the script this obvious everywhere? Are you willing to look at it? To take it to heart?

The writers of the script are making the "mystery" a little thin, no?

Convenience and the Script

The script hands you a culture of convenience which is leading toward a culture that has less capability to think, move, and defend itself. You might say it is being domesticated.

M Mice?

D Duck?

R Squirrel?

G Dog?

A Ant?

:)

So least resistance is M Donald's (Duck?), etc.

Don't you find the script a little claustrophobic?

Why?

What is the point?

My motivation is my own.

My visions are my own. As yours are yours.

I am doing this because an enslaved culture that is being domesticated is docile unless it realizes that it is being domesticated.

As Neo sort of said: "I am not hear to tell you what is next. I am hear to show the world something. I am here to show the world the 'men' behind the curtain pulling the levers and writing the lines. I am here to show the slaves their collars. And the walls of their pen. As written by you."

The fact that your pen is.

Pen is.

The pen is mightier than the sword. The Spoken word.

Whose Pen Is are we discussing and where is it in your life?

The Genesis and Endnote

This work would not have been possible without the work of John M. Allegro, who deserves great praise for the Sacred Mushroom and The Cross. Without that book I would not have thought about the connection between the Lebanese Cedar tree and the amanita muscaria mushroom and the dominant holiday's big symbols, the Christmas tree and the Santa Claus (or the little red and white packages under the tree).

To much editing is a pain and kills the raw channeled work, therefore I have left the text somewhat raw.

I write and it comes to me. I don't know where it comes from except it fits. So connections that are wonderous, even to me, just jump onto the page.

Like the Why page. The section on what the Pen Is literally occured on the page.

In a similar light Penn's Woods is a penis landscape. And Jello Biafra and the DK's got shafted for obscenity for their penis landscape in Frankenchrist. /giggle again!/ NPFO, indeed!

Does Woody have a Buzz or does Buzz have a Woody? It's a Toy Story either way.

Happiness in Pursuit

Some folks ha penis and some folks don't ha penis. They ha vagina. Too simple? How do you create a circumstance to encode that women will never ever be treated as equal and never ever get the joke?

Write it out in the program, the language!

So ladies, no more pursuit of ha penis, eh?

Maybe a homophone like ha Venus?

See the matrix, cut the matrix's pen off at the base?

The matrix ain't a Mother, its a little boy who never wants to meet a woman, so he wrote their development out of possibility.

Nice!

Time to change!

:)

In Summary

During the last few weeks of 2014 I have been trying to think of a way to tie this first book together. I would say it is what I see, how my life and insides sees what is being offered as a life to live.

What is being offered is the best barbaric unkind brutal and horrible life imaginable. At every single turn the choice has been made to turn away from treating people nicely or treating the land with respect and instead either putting a knife in their back or burning the land and sky.

It is a refinement on foolish waste and perverse sadomasachistic behavior. Human diet is a physiological certainty, don't eat animals. Choice: screw that. Invent controversy. Eat salt (read the simple soils addendum if you have quetions on biological life's reaction to the addition of salt.).

I wish I could be complimentary about some aspect of the mass experience. I can't be. The Vedas offer recipes with salt via Ayurveda, so the Vedas be damned, they are anti-life. Buddhism wishes us to conquer our desires, when what is required is a full life's experience. But life is long.

So in summary. Everything I see is a lowest level catering to the lowest common denominator.

McDonald's delivered to the Penthouse of the Four Seasons.

I can't involve myself with such a penis worshipping collection of shit. So I will be putting my effort into removing this society and putting together something more reasonable. I have lots and lots of lives to spend doing it.

Bonus Content: Simple Soils

(This addendum was added because it is useful information that appeared first in Brian Rossiter's Fruit Powered online magazine in November of 2014 and it makes the document long enough for create space.)

This document presents the commonly understood concept: A simple definition of soil.

This concept allows us to sow and grow a plant and understand: What food is.

What soil is and how it grows plant foods is a simple but powerful foundation from which one can generate: The mandate for everyone to farm, The mandate to feed everyone food, and The mandate to decentralize.

Soil is rich in life. It is maintained using biological organic material that is returned to it by its maintainers. In a mature biological system, plant and animal bodies and rock would litter the ground and act as a food source for a web of soil life.

(Understanding the soil life web concerns Dr. Elaine Ingham,

Jeff Lowenfels and Robert Cannard. Their reference material is available on YouTube and beyond.)

Soil is alive, and in that way, it differs from dirt, which has no life in it. In fact, soil has billions of organisms per teaspoon, from the bacterial and viral to worms and insects.

This life web is created by adding organic material to dirt along with inorganic material or rock or rock dusts. The soil life, or its digestive system, springs to life from compost and teas that one can add to bring the dirt to life. The organic material can be simply plants grown in place that are allowed to return to the Earth after they have enjoyed the full completeness of their life. After this cycle has been repeated many times, soil begins to have a healthy digestive system with its ready access to abundant mineral rock, air, water and light.

This soil is the living skin of our Earth, our Gaia, if you will.

The soil's digestion is home to fungi, bacteria, nematoads, insects, worms and many other life forms.

Soil building is the key because with healthy soil growing, grwoing healthy plants is reasonably easy.

Plants grow by drawing water up from their main roots through their bodies and transpiring, or sweating, it out of their leaves. Photosynthesis in the leaves creates simple sugars that the plant uses a fraction of to grow and send another fraction back down to its roots—not the main roots, but to the hair roots. These sugars are exuded by the plants' hair roots with messages to the soil flora that the plant would like a certain nutrient or set of nutrients. The soil flora set about obtaining those nutrients in exchange for more sugars. This sets up a mining and exchange system in which the plants use sugars to drive the behaviors of the soil fauna, which use the products of the sugar metabolism (acids) to dissolve rocks and obtain the available minerals.

These minerals are surrendered to the plant when the soil fauna dies and are swept up by the vacuuming action of the plant drinking. In this way, the plant can be seen as a carnivore, eating the protoplasmic soup of dead soil fauna, which it offered sugars to earlier. This transport is sometimes against osmotic pressure in order to stockpile them for future use. The influence of the plant on the local area is immense as the fungi area can be many miles in extent, covering resources and using exchanges of all the mineral sources in the area as well as the plants in the area that exude different sugars to mine (possibly) foods that are not directly available to a given plant but only available in such a vibrant community.

Quoting Bob Cannard: "Carrots concentrate gold in their bodies, and it is not understood why this happens; it does not happen for other plants on the whole, just for carrots. But if one plants seed of whatever plant and does not supply everything that the plant could possibly want, gold and silver and everything in between, one cannot be sure that the plant's needs are being met. When a plant's needs are fully met, its immune system is able to defend it, and pests are not a problem, and the resulting fruit has an etheric sweetness and vitality that provides us with the same capability to generate our own best potential."

This plant has all of its needs met that we are able to understand and many more that we do not understand at all but that we have allowed for by supplying absolutely everything we can.

This total process is a conscious one. Plants have been seen as being alive, but with this simple but correct understanding, they are acknowledged as conscious beings.

If the soil is disturbed by tilling, etc., air is introduced and the flora and fauna are oxidized, and they die. The fragile fungi networks are broken—certainly they can regrow, but there are costs. From this, one can reflect on the lifestyle that would result from pedantically treating Gaia's skin as being sacred, to be maintained and never pierced.

The society that would grow up is one without metals, petroleum, fossil fuels, etc. Solar, wind and renewable energies sources would be the norm.

These considerations can be thought about, if you like, and

they are interesting. Their proposal is contained here, but their discussion is not. The way the Earth has been used is also the product of the culture, which is one of domination, not one of long-term consideration, compassion and planning.

At this point, we have defined what soil is. The soil's digestion, with access to abundant rock, water, air and light, will grow healthy plants at the lowest cost to the farmer and society. This low cost is achieved by having everyone be the healthiest they can be and being able to fully contribute in the community.

This food is the least quality level that is acceptable for humans. It is possible to envision better soil with dedication of farmers and society to this way of life.

Since we require a society that is doing its best, it is not possible to condone having anyone be allowed to consume a lesser-quality food item. Food is basic to human dignity, and every human has the right to dignity.

If someone did not have enough food today, he or she would not be able to be at his or her best. We would be consciously saying, "So and so does not have to be at their best; therefore, society does not have to be at its best, and, as a result, I do not have to be at my best."

With this simple understanding, it is no longer acceptable for the food industry to continue to perform in the economically *more* expensive and soil-destructive manner that it presently does. It is only acceptable for it to change and for basic food to be freely available to everyone to make the whole community the best it can be.

To do anything else breaks our agreement to be at our best.

Explicitly, it is obvious that the liabilities in growing substandard food for market will destroy the current agricultural model. Since you see its days as being numbered, you understand whose responsibility your food growing becomes. Yes, look in the mirror and greet the farmer newly born.

Historically, what are the reasons behind the poisonous practices of industrial farming?

If soil is not constantly renewed, it will stop producing prodigious health-giving food after a number of years. In that case, what farmers have done for many a day is to either abandon the land for more fertile ground or switch crops to one that does not need as fertile ground. After many cycles, the Earth is depleted and the original crop types are not even attempted anymore, only the crops that do well in soils that are barely alive are grown. At that point, it is tempting to rebuild the soil by growing a goodly fraction of the plants for the expressed purpose of soil regeneration. But if this information about the nature of soil and the true long-term costs is hidden, then greedy dominating parties can sell a philosophy of never-ending poisoning. This is the philosophy of today's industrial agriculture in which the land crops are grown exclusively for human needs and the needs of the soil, and thus the plants are not considered. As you can see, not to consider the needs of the soil and the plants is to ignore our own needs. And not be our best.

Industrial agriculture tempts farmers with soluble fertilizers in which the nutrition is a salt. This salt dissolves directly in groundwater and is drunk by the plants in an involuntary, nonconscious manner. It is involuntary precisely because the plant must drink. The growth of these salted plants is remarkable. They grow quite quickly, and the size of the fruit is much larger than food. This is because the plant is growing much faster than it should, which is driven by the very few nutrients it does receive as salty nutrition. The bloated plant is sickly due to the salty poison it has been forced to drink. The word "poison" is used here to contrast these growing conditions, in salted dirt, from those present in healthy soil.

The groundwater is poisoned with this salty fertilizer, and this salt is washed away very soon, leaving the plant gasping for nutrition in dirt as the soil is not alive and able to bring the plant what it needs. So more fertilizer is required. More poison.

This sickly plant and crop does not develop its immune system to completeness and is vulnerable to pests. In fact, Gaia tests each plant to assess its fitness. These tests come in the form of insect, animal and plant "pests." With the correct nutrition, healthy plants have no issues with pests but when raised in poison, the outcome of being challenged is obvious. The sickly plant is eaten by pests.

Many so-called pests are beneficial to plants. Sickly plants are certainly removed, but there are many examples where pests live in concert with the healthy plants and eat old leaves and detritus matter, returning their own rich compost to the base of the plants. Thus, when the plant is healthy, the pest lives as it should as a helper.

The loss of the sickly plant could trigger the farmer to remediate the soil and begin to build it to grow healthy crops, but in industrial agricultural practice, it triggers spraying of crops with pesticides and herbicides. In short, these thrice-poisoned sickly plants are brought to market today and passed off as food fit for humans. It is completely obvious that this is not the case.

So why does it happen? It is because of a lack of information and the presence of debt that farmers see no alternative to the poisoning and to delivering poisoned crops as if they were food. This is not a happy life for farmers, for plants, for soils, for anyone.

If you are reading these words, it is no longer the case that you are ignorant of these basic life facts. Maybe you were not ignorant of them before. It is now the society's priority to provide only food and not poison called food. It is also not possible to allow food to be shipped many thousands of miles to arrive at your door having lost its freshness. Everything is now local. Your complete food table can no longer be more than a day distant from you.

Agriculture is now squarely in the hands of the small grower. But much more than that, it is the direct responsibility of every individual to grow his or her own calorie staple crop in his or her own yard, windowsill or rooftop. And it is not enough to grow for yourself and to be content. One can be content only when we know that everyone has had enough to eat tonight. That no one has gone to bed hungry. And that everyone has eaten food, locally grown food from the neighborhood yards and growers who everyone knows.

When everyone is together for a meal, it is time to discuss how to make better soils, crops, people, etc. It is time to discuss social models, behavior modes, philosophy, art, etc.

This is the least acceptable standard for society. The lowest setting of the bar. Not one bit of the present standard is acceptable. The present archetype is not the worship and affirmation of life, it is the opposite.

What soil is and, as a result, what food is was the purpose of this simple letter. The information in it is very basic, but since society is still structured in an obsolete way, it is a call to action. At this time in history, action cannot be avoided if humans wish to remain on Earth. But even with low population and verdant soils, why would you insist on proceeding along the path of lesser performance if you knew better?

You know better now.

Do not hesitate to become more informed about soil health through the work of Elaine Ingham, Jeff Lowenfels, Robert Cannard and many others. Find your way to the knowledge and wisdom contained in permaculture in the works of Bill Mollison, Geoff Lawton and many others.

And remember, unlike the present social structure, the new social structure is completely local and, as such, local idiosyncrasies will lead to local products that will be unique, not staple crops or basic goods but fine fabric, art, etc. using local renewable resources into which the local region pours its love.

The time of the society of domination is over. The experiment called "Rule from the Center" brought us to this point and now is the time to prioritize food and water standards as being basic in our lives, to our lives, and to our communities.

That our next-door neighbor is getting enough to eat and is eating well cannot be his or her private concern if he or she is not performing well. Bring everyone to the table at mealtime. We need every hand and every perspective.

There are many other insights that can be achieved, now that this basic information is understood.

****

Questions:

What is soil? Compare that with what dirt is.

What regenerative steps can be taken to change dirt into soil?

How is nutrition consciously gathered by plants in soil?

What are the three stages of poisons added in industrial agriculture to bring that crop to market?

Where must all crops be grown from now on so that they are fresh to our table?

When must these changes to society be undertaken?

Where must each individual plant his or her own food crops and whose well-being is everyone responsible for?

****

Plants transpire water from their leaves. They sweat. Dogs, cats, pigs and cows, to name a few animals, control their body temperature not by sweating but by panting or wallowing or with other methods.

So in effect, one group of living conscious beings (plants, humans, primates, horses, giraffes, etc.) sweat and, in doing so, contribute moisture to the atmosphere, resulting in rain or condensation some time later. They are rainmakers.

By comparing sweating, human beings are much more closely related to plants than to dogs and cats and pigs.

Questions:

Does it stand to reason that humans, like plants, like their nutrients as a solution of salt or in plant form where they can be acquired or rejected voluntarily?

This conclusion that soluble salt is anathema to life has implications.

Consuming salt becomes an emergency-only measure and should never happen in anything other than the most acute situations. All culinary, medical, social traditions and knowledge sources that mandate, prescribe or propose adding soluble salt nutrients to a meal or preparation must be questioned to their core. It is not enough to change part of the philosophy. The philosophy has been found to be a death practice because it advocates adding salt. It is only in the examination and rejection of each philosophy and directive springing from the past culture of domination that one can become free of it.

This consideration explicitly challenges Ayurveda.

This consideration explicitly challenges Allopathic medical practices.

I sincerely hope you as a reader of this document take what it says seriously. I take it very seriously as its implicatyons mean that society needs to change for be something closer to a living model and not a dying model.

Drastic changes are not required. Grow some of your food. Understand what soil is and figure out how to change your dirt to soil. Understand that governments are not imterested in critically thinking local civic structure, they are interested in vast demographics of the mentally handicapped, malnourished, confused, ignorant zombies.

In that realization you see where we head.

Bon Voyage!

www.ingramcontent.com/pod-product-compliance
Lightning Source LLC
Chambersburg PA
CBHW062105270326
41931CB00013B/3223